BOXING

BY

PERCY LONGHURST

CONTENTS

CHAPTER		PAGE
I.	FIRST PRINCIPLES	5
II.	HITTING AND LEADING	14
III.	COUNTER TO LEADS	24
IV.	FEINTING: THE DOUBLE LEAD AND ONE-TWO	36
V.	IN-FIGHTING	48
VI.	TRAINING	57

CHAPTER I

FIRST PRINCIPLES

THE boxer whose knowledge of the art is founded on the mastery of the principles of what is called the English style, as taught by such instructors as Ned Donnelly, Abe Daltrey, and Bat Mullins, has no need to be ashamed of his knowledge, or to regret that he has not been instructed according to the modern methods of glove fighting of which American, French, and other Continental boxers are the exponents.

So far as professional boxing is concerned, no Englishman is the holder of a world's title. As to amateur boxing, at the Olympic Games of Paris, 1924, with 29 countries competing, the British team secured First and Second in the Middle weights, First in the Light Heavy, Second in the Fly weight, and but for the injury to the hands of its Heavies' representative, would almost certainly have figured in that final ; a record surpassed only by the U.S.A., which won two Firsts, two Seconds, and two Thirds.

The average glove fighter knows little or nothing of genuine boxing. His methods are unpleasant to watch and bear scant resemblance to the boxing art. Straight, clean hitting he despises—or has never learned; he relies on wild, vicious swings with either hand, some of which he is hopeful may get home. Most of them are wasted on the air. His footwork, upon which the genuine boxer relies for both attack and defence, is all but nil. He is an adept at clinching, roughing, holding, lying on and mauling his opponent, preventing him from doing any clean work. So long as he hits his adversary somewhere, and hard, he appears to be quite satisfied.

This is modern glove fighting at its worst; and this worst is being taken as a model by a disagreeably large number of the amateur boxers of to-day. That it does *not* succeed when its user comes up against a strong, determined adversary, quick and hard-hitting, who has been trained in the principles of the older school, who keeps his head and refuses to be intimidated by wild slogging and unfair devices, is an assertion not to be successfully contradicted.

Professional Methods

The system of modern glove fighting is not that which is to the advantage of the man or youth to whom boxing is not the means of livelihood but an athletic exercise, a recreation, a form of physical training bringing both pleasure and profit, and, in addition, a self defensive art upon which he may be able to rely if called upon to secure his bodily safety against a chance assault. It is for him that the present treatise is intended.

FIRST PRINCIPLES

"To hit and not to be hit," is the terse phrase in which is crystallised the sum of the principles of skilled boxing. The accomplishment of this double feat is the whole science of boxing in a nutshell.

To defeat your opponent—whether your best friend, who is obliging you with a three rounds bout, or a rough who presumes on his physical advantages or has designs on your health or your pocket—you have to be near enough to him to hit him—and not to hit him only once and hard, but hard and often, and to keep on doing so; and to achieve this you must take the risk of his hitting you.

To Escape Being Hit

And here indeed is one of the very first things the novice boxer has to learn—that to avoid being hit (the idea which is uppermost in the minds of most novices), it is not necessary to take and try to maintain a position two or three yards away from the opponent.

To stand six feet away from your man means that you have to make an entirely unnecessary effort to reach him; which is waste of energy. Given the knowledge how to defend yourself, you are as safe six inches beyond his reach as at six feet. I say "given the knowledge"; to provide that knowledge is the purpose of boxing. For it should never be forgotten that boxing is the art of self defence.

This advice is given with a full appreciation of the

truth existing in the old ring maxim that "attack is the best defence." It is—sometimes; but to neglect the defensive side of the art is to lay the foundations of receiving, one day, a very complete and disagreeable surprise.

Fig. 1. The right way to guard a left at head.

Evidences of such neglect—the outcome of eagerness to imitate the hit-at-any-price methods of the professional glove fighter which is so deplorable —are obvious enough in modern amateur boxing. The fault is largely responsible for so many amateur bouts seen to-day being nothing more than mere

FIRST PRINCIPLES

rough-and-tumble scrambling encounters, devoid of science and real interest. It leads to that blot on modern boxing—persistent clinching and holding. Never having learned to defend himself properly, the modern boxer is far too apt to go into a clinch, to hold his opponent and hang on, simply to avoid getting hurt. He attacks furiously, misses his objective, and at once resorts to hugging because he is aware of no other method of extricating himself, from the awkward position wherein he finds himself, except at the risk of being hit.

Body Movements

Nature has provided only one means of assaulting an adversary—the fists, but she has given two whereby such assault may be negatived or evaded—the arms and the legs. To these boxing art has added a third—the skilful swaying or moving the body above the hips either backwards or sideways. Not a great number of amateurs acquire this knack; some professionals master it; and its employment is one of the prettiest of boxing feats.

Some persons seem to think that the learning of the knack is a matter to be deferred until after a general knowledge of the boxing art has been acquired—that only long experience will give it. The writer does not agree. To him there appears no reason why the learner should not come to understand how simple can be made the evasion of a blow by carrying the target, the head or body, away from it without troubling to move the feet even to the extent of an inch.

Footwork

The novice usually has more difficulty in managing his feet than his hands, possibly due to the fact that leg action with most of us is more automatic than arm action. Directly a number of steps have to be taken quickly one man in three will be seen to be in trouble with his feet.

The novice fails to realise how important it is that his feet should be under control—the control frequent practice will develop. Such practice need not be confined to those periods when an opponent is facing him. He should practise footwork during spare moments or when exercising with the punch ball.

The distance the feet are apart will vary with one's height. The old standard of 14 inches for a boxer of 5ft. 8ins. is a safe guide. The legs should be only slightly bent; avoid the exaggerated bending that accompanies the American crouch, in which, too, more than its proportion of weight is thrown on one leg. But never "lock" the knee joints. To do so means stiffness, ungainliness, and slowness of movement. From neck to heels there should be no stiffness, no "setting" of the muscles. Even the hands should be half open, not clenched. The time for hard clenching of the glove comes just before a blow is delivered. Keep every joint and muscle loose and easy.

FIRST PRINCIPLES

The left foot ought to point directly forward, the right making a half turn to its right. If the learner will also bear in mind that the foot to be moved first is always that already nearest the direction to which he intends moving, he will not find himself in the dangerous position of " crossed legs," in which it will be an easy matter for him to be knocked down. Move first the left when advancing, the right when retreating.

By keeping the advanced foot pointing forward, not across—one of the novice's bugbears—there is avoided the likelihood of your advance being checked by collision with your opponent's advanced leg.

To move to the right, let the right foot move first and not too far, say six or eight inches, the other following up at once. For a left movement, start with the left foot. By this means the feet preserve their relative position.

Practise all these movements, in your bedroom, when sparring with your gym. friends, and they will soon become quite easy to you. Move slowly at first, then quicker; don't raise the feet high and move as easily and quietly as possible.

As a general rule, when on the move, unless directly attacking, let your movement be to your opponent's left. The natural tendency towards your own left hand must be mastered, as this will bring you within reach of opponent's right hand.

If you don't learn how to move to your advantage, should you be forced against the ropes you'll have a bad time. In such position, *always* slip away to your right; and if with this sidestep you combine a rightward ducking of the head, you may not only escape unscathed but you will have the chance, if quick, of getting home heavily on the unprotected left side of your opponent, which will be turned towards you.

Fig. 2. Side-stepping a left lead at head and countering with right.

How to Sidestep

The sidestep is one of the most simple and easy methods of evading an intended blow, yet one sees it employed but comparatively seldom. Some instructors appear to think it an advanced movement

FIRST PRINCIPLES 13

for which the learner is not ready until many lessons have gone by. I entirely disagree. No particular skill is necessary, only reasonably careful timing. The weight is placed momentarily upon the left foot (heel raised slightly), and with a half spring, half step, to your right, and a slight body turn, you have not only evaded opponent's rush and his threatening left hand, but you are " outside " him ; his clear view of you is broken, and, your left foot brought up to the front again, you are admirably placed for a telling retaliation at his left side, completely exposed to you.

The effect is twofold, moral as well as physical. It gives the learner confidence by proving to him how simply the purpose of a headlong rush that threatens to overwhelm him may be frustrated ; and the development of confidence means also the development of coolness and clearheadedness, of which the average learner (the writer hasn't forgotten his own going through the mill !) stands so much in need.

Successful employment of the hands depends so largely upon the proper use and control of the feet that all the practice of the latter it is possible to get cannot but give good results. To ignore or neglect footwork is sheer folly, a hindrance to progress. It may not be so exciting as exchanging buffets with a fellow enthusiast, but it is of infinite value ; and its benefits will at once become apparent when, some idea of correct hitting having been gained, bouts of sparring, loose play, are indulged in.

The use of the feet having been mastered, the other half of the business, hitting and guarding, is very much more easily and rapidly picked up; for the reason that the brain will have so much the less with which to concern itself.

CHAPTER II

Hitting and Leading

AGAIN and again is it asserted that boxing can never be learned from a book. Such is true enough —to the extent that no boxer can be made merely by reading what he should do. A complete theoretical knowledge of how to hit, guard, parry, counter, and use the feet is of no use unless there is plenty of actual glove practice. The purpose of the book is to indicate the lines upon which the learner is to study his subject; to make clear to him what is best to do in given circumstances. The book is useful in pointing out the certain mistakes that will be made, but it cannot take the place of actual boxing.

With the help of a book the learner can avoid doing those things which will prevent his becoming a good boxer. If it is a worthy one, there is no reason why the novice who follows its instruction should not be as successful as was Sapper O'Neill, Lightweight Army and Navy champion before the

HITTING AND LEADING

Great War, and a man who held his own for ten rounds against the world's champion.

O'Neill got hold of such a book while a youngster; and day after day he would practise by himself, in front of a looking glass so as to make sure of following the instructions quite accurately, mastering the forms of straight hitting, of accurate guarding, of footwork, ducking etc. The result was that when he found someone with whom he could put on the gloves, he knew already what he *ought* to do, and his chief work was to try to put that knowledge into active effort.

Straight Hitting

Straight hitting is perhaps the most difficult part of the boxing art to master; the want of it is the most commonly seen boxing fault. It is not a natural action; the natural tendency is to hit round or with a chopping action, or else merely to push the arm forward.

It is difficult to get some boxers to admit, or to understand, that the really straight hit is the hardest blow that can be dealt, that is to say, the most punishing. And in boxing one does need to hit hard—the harder the better. At least, we'll say that one wants to know *how* to hit hard. Even in the friendliest of bouts, the hitting should not be merely tapping.

The straight hit, properly delivered, is the most severe because it is quicker than the swinging or chopping kind, and because it is possible to get behind it the best part of all one's body weight. A swinging blow may be a hard one, as behind it will be some, but not all, of the available body weight; but it is not safe because the part of the hand that receives the shock is not that part which can take a severe shock without the risk of being damaged in the process.

With a swing, the impact falls upon the smaller knuckles of the fist. Clench your fist, swing it from outwards and across, and prove to yourself which will be the part of the hands first to come into collision with the object struck.

Now shoot out your arm, fist closed tightly, elbow underneath, hand turned so that the palm is chiefly uppermost. Note that the impact is taken by the knuckles at the bases of the fingers. The wrist is straight, the elbow joint is locked in the complete straightening of the arm behind, and there is a straight line direct from the striking point to the shoulder. In a swing you will already have noted, in addition to where the impact of the blow is taken, that the arm is somewhen bent when the blow is actually made.

How a Blow Should be Struck

Now, these facts being noticed, it should not be difficult to understand that the straight arm blow will be harder than the swinging one, because the one is represented as at the end of a straight and

HITTING AND LEADING

perfectly rigid line (the bones of the arm), while the latter is at the end of a bent line, formed by the bent elbow. The trouble is that the straight hit is not always properly delivered; there is not the forward movement and, in consequence, not the whole of the body weight behind it. Too often it is little better than a poke or jab, the force of which comes only from the arm itself as it is extended.

I am not telling you, however, that the force of a blow, its power " to hurt," depends entirely upon its being a straight drive. Other factors enter into that—condition and development of the striker's muscles; the speed at which the fist is travelling; and whether the receiver of the blow is moving towards it or away from it when the glove meets him; all these count.

Faults of the Swinging Blow

One other point against the swinging blow you will at once understand without any explanation—it encourages the tendency to hit with the open glove, or, if not that, the front of the glove. Such hitting in a serious encounter would be pure waste of time. In competitive boxing it is also worthless, because no points are awarded for " slapping " or " flicking," as reference to the rules shows.

Positions for Hitting

The old time instructors were very insistent

upon the position of the hands and arms when delivering the various blows. This was reckoned at least as important as the manner of carrying the arms when sparring for an opening and also when guarding.

They had reason on their side. They had had experience of round arm hitting (a hundred years ago, the majority of the P. R. fighters knew nothing of straight hitting), and its weaknesses and faults had been proved to them. Straight hitting became the characteristic of English boxing science.

To-day, it is not so. Boxers have retrograded; they have gone back from the improved principles and to the bent arm hitting of a hundred years ago. Also, to-day, injuries to the hands, dislocation of thumbs, driving up of knuckles, are more prevalent than they were with the skilled knuckle fighters with whom straight hitting was a fetish.

It is argued that principles suited to knuckle fighting do not apply to boxing. And in the matter of hitting the argument is wholly fallacious. Hitting is hitting, whether the hands be gloved or not, and anatomical principles remain the same to-day as fifty years back.

Let the novice give careful study to the drawings illustrating the hand positions and afterwards try to imitate them in his practice.

The first shows the position when leading off with the left hand.

The second shows the position for a right hand cross counter. It is identical with the fourth, which

HITTING AND LEADING 19

shows how a right hand body blow should be made, which is also a retaliatory, not an attacking, blow.

The third indicates position for a left hand body hit.

Practise these blows a few times, the hands held

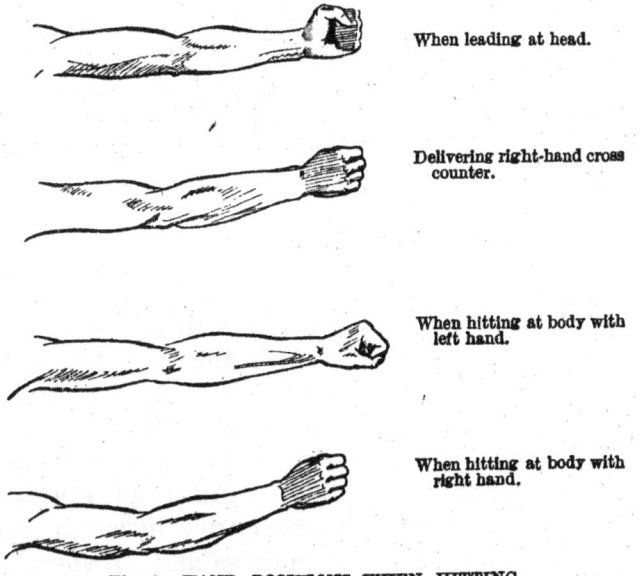

Fig. 3. HAND POSITIONS WHEN HITTING.

thus; then make similar movements with the hands held otherwise. The first will feel easy and comfortable; you will at once appreciate the readiness and force with which the ensuing blow will be given. The second series of attempts will be cramped, ineffective, weak by comparison.

Practise the correct blows again and again, following O'Neill's method if you like, until the manner becomes a habit. Keep the moves in your mind when sparring. You will develop straight hitting, a hard punch, and can rest assured your hands will be little likely to become damaged.

Hitting as the old instructors advised, you will the more readily understand the importance of the tried maxim insisting upon the elbows being kept in. Carry the elbows outward and upward (you must do that for a swinging blow) and you at once expose your ribs.

The Upper Cut

There is one blow that the novice will learn for which, even when made in the orthodox manner, a bent arm is necessary. It is the upper cut—supposed to have been invented by that hard-hitting old pugilist of Regency times, Dutch Sam.

It is not a leading blow. It is a blow to be used at close-quarter fighting or against an adversary who rushes in head down—a trick in which some modern boxers (?) will indulge and to which the rough-and-tumble fighter is very prone.

The arm is bent (right hand upper cut is best), forearm at right angles, face of the hand towards the striker, and the fist shot upwards to meet opponent's face or stomach. There should be a quick straightening of the right leg, a thrusting forward of the body, as the hit is made, thus adding to its force. The

HITTING AND LEADING

elbow must be kept down, not allowed to stray outward, or most of the force of the blow will be lost.

THE LEFT-HAND LEAD

Now, after much preliminary, we come to the left-hand lead, the orthodox attack, and usually a boxer's first offensive movement. Until he has gathered knowledge and experience, he must regard his left hand as his attacking weapon; it is the points gatherer. The right hand and arm are for guarding, also supplementing the efforts of its fellow by taking advantage of openings in the adversary's defence that have been caused by left hand use.

Unless the novice be careful to bear in mind all the essentials of a good left-hand attack, he, trying to carry into effect what he understands of straight hitting, will fall into the mistake of merely poking with his left instead of hitting. His left arm is extended, bent, elbow turned in but not cramped, fist at about the level of his own chin and with the thumb edge uppermost. From that position he has to carry his hand straight forward and reach his opponent's face with a force sufficient to be felt.

This is not easy. A simple extension of the arm will result only in a mild prod—if the glove land. It will not be much more however quick the movement; and the hand itself is not to be drawn back so that a greater impetus may be gained. How then may the required force be obtained?

The answer is—Utilisation of the body weight.

The learner with the gloves on for the first few times has a mighty respect for his opponent's fists. He comprehends that by getting near enough to connect with his left glove, he runs the risk of opponent's glove connecting with *his* face.

Of course, his guard arm should prevent that ; that is part of its job ; and as the left glove is shoved forward the right arm, from the position of defence shown, is to be carried upwards, maintaining its line of direction—not too high—the top of glove about level with the upper edge of the forehead—so that if opponent's left is sent forward, it will be intercepted, caught on the outside of the arm and turned aside. The movement is worth independent practice, one party leading at the head, raising the guard simultaneously, the other simply guarding.

But the novice is not too confident of his guard, and when he leads out with his left, his tendency is to bend the rear knee and throw upon it most of his weight as he takes back his head and shoulders. Obviously this is wrong. If the head and shoulders are moving back while the fist is moving in the contrary direction, the fist cannot reach its objective, owing to the backward pull on the arm, and the power behind it will be about nil.

So to get what is wanted the novice has to learn to do several things. A little of the power of the blow comes from the arm muscles, most from the weight behind it ; therefore, instead of the head and shoulders going back, the rear knee bending,

HITTING AND LEADING

the reverse movements must be made. The left foot should be advanced, say sixteen inches or so, a quick, sliding movement; the right heel is raised and the right leg straightened, thus propelling the body forward; while an actual forward movement of the body from the hips upward takes place. The left shoulder is turned forward with the body movement and the arm sharply straightened. The net result, entirely apart from the added force with which the fist meets the object aimed at is that the glove is carried almost 30 inches further than by the halting, half-hearted, incorrect attempt, previously mentioned.

Thirty inches! Let the learner try to realise what this means.

The practice necessary to perform correctly this attack which the learner can get during a lesson from the instructor, or if put up against another learner, is not sufficient for the complete movement to be quickly mastered. But if the enthusiastic novice will practise the movement on his own at odd times, progress will be much more rapid, and his lesson from the intructor become of far greater value. A mark on a wall will serve well enough as his target.

Largely because sufficient practice is not indulged in, the method of making the ideal left-hand attack is never wholly mastered by some boxers. The matter is simply one of taking pains. Success will come with application; and the fellow who really means to become a boxer will not grudge this, knowing that his mastery of the left hand attack will make him an opponent to be respected in any boxing company.

CHAPTER III

Counter to Leads

PROFICIENCY with the left-hand lead gives its owner inestimable advantages. He can spar around his adversary, pick his opportunity, shoot in his blow and spring back again without the other having much chance of touching him. Such boxing allows a light boxer to defeat one much heavier than himself. Again, successful leading allows a boxer to dominate his opponent, to set the pace, to lay down the lines on which the contest is to be fought.

The guard against the left lead is the pushing upwards of the right hand glove. The slower the hit is made, the easier is it for defender to parry and also make a return hit.

Aware of what is coming, the defender, not satisfied merely to stop the blow with his guard arm or get out of danger by drawing back his head (no need to shift the feet to do this, remember!), as he interposes his guard, will also shoot forward his left hand. If he is a bit quicker than attacker, the latter not only fails to get home but possibly receives a flush hit full in the face. If the counter land, it will do so with very great force, as the collision between two objects moving towards each other—face and defender's glove—is much more severe than when one of the objects is stationary.

Fig. 4. A Stop Hit with right at head replying to slow left lead.

A slow left lead may also be well met by a stop hit with right at head—if you are quick enough.

Left-Hand Counter

The left-hand counter is a most excellent move

for the novice, but the best form of it is not always explained to him by even a competent teacher. Usually he is recommended to do no more than shoot his glove forward ; but this is not enough. Done properly, the left counter can be made so telling the recipient is not only checked but well punished and his confidence weakened.

To make the counter aright requires an understanding of the best method of guarding with the right arm. The older professors insisted the right should be placed diagonally across the body, elbow down, forearm covering the mark, fist over the left breast. The better way is to have the arm away from the body, elbow down, of course, glove well away from the chest. The left arm is forward, not fully extended, and its fist is pointing straight to opponent's chin. The position of the right arm should be such that a straight line drawn along the forearm and through the fist, if continued, would meet the centre of the palm of the left hand.

This position does away with the stiffness of the older form of guard ; it makes the right arm more mobile, the fist more ready for use and quicker in its action. When guarding, the right is merely carried upwards (still keeping the elbow down), the forearm maintaining the same line of direction, so that opponent's left meets it and glances down the outside. Such a guard is less likely to leave the forearm bruised than was the old style one. This action of the arm carries with it the whole of the shoulder ; so that the right shoulder moves

COUNTER TO LEADS

forward and the left one is correspondingly drawn back.

Now when the left-hand counter comes to be made, this drawing back of the left shoulder does much to add to the force of the blow. There has been the slight shoulder swing in one direction as the guard is made; it is followed immediately by a corresponding swing in the other direction as the left arm shoots forward for the counter, making the blow more punishing than it would be if coming from a stationary shoulder, as must be the case with the blow delivered in accordance with the older method of guarding. Moreover, the reach is slightly increased by the body twist, thus making more probable the reaching of opponent's head.

One of the finest exponents of this modern method of guarding and left hand countering was the late Jim Driscoll; opponents as well as onlookers were mystified by the ease and certainty with which, time after time, he would carry aside a threatening left lead at his head and, seemingly without any serious effort, reply at once with a punishing counter.

That the efficacy of such countering depends upon the manner of guarding will be at once realised; and there seems no reason whatever why the novice taking his first lesson in guarding should not learn this method rather than the more orthodox one that is usually taught him.

Any real boxing bout, even between two learners, is a contest of wits as well as of arms and legs. However proficient one may become with the left-hand lead, to confine oneself to a persistent repetition thereof will result in the object being defeated. By continually doing the same thing in the same way, you acquaint your opponent with your intentions; he knows what you'll do and prepares accordingly. Therefore, it is well, the left-hand lead mastered, to introduce something new. This may be either a feint or a duck.

Ducking

Ducking is simply a removal of the head to get it out of the way of a possible counter. Well done, it is most effective, puzzling and probably annoying opponent.

To combine a duck with your left lead. This involves your being closer to opponent than when you intend to launch an ordinary left lead. The reason is that although your left foot goes forward you don't cover so much ground. Instead of springing from your right forefoot, the foot remains flat on the floor. So gradually decrease distance between self and opponent, moving in a few inches at a time until you judge the right distance has been arrived at. Advance left foot quickly, and as you lead off, move your head so as to avoid opponent's left glove as he tries to counter or hit with his left. Slipping is really a better word than ducking, for the head movement is really a sideways and slightly forward one, so that opponent's arm slips past the side of your head. Ducking is actually the lowering of the head so as to allow opponent's

COUNTER TO LEADS

glove to pass over it. Straight hits are slipped; swinging or hooking blows are ducked.

Confidence is necessary for this move, simple as it is, as the movement should not take place until opponent's glove is quite near your face.

Fig. 5. Position ready for attack or defence.

The head movement is best made to the right—your right—so that opponent's glove passes over your left shoulder. In any case, the movement should be of a few inches only; otherwise, the body movement is interfered with and the left lead probably spoiled.

A useful point to note : When slipping or ducking, don't shut the eyes—a common fault.

This head slipping may be usefully employed as a purely defensive measure. Instead of parrying a straight left at the head, as you shift the head, launch a left-hand counter at attacker's body or

Fig. 6. Ducking to right from a left lead, and countering with left to jaws.

jaw. The sideways movement imparted by the shifting of the head to the right automatically causes the left shoulder to come forward, and the left hand drive at the body for a counter is an almost natural expedient.

Slipping to the left has one advantage : it paves

the way towards effective use of one of the most notable of all boxing blows, fascinating and most tremendously effective—the Right-hand Cross Counter.

RIGHT-HAND CROSS COUNTER

This is not an easy blow, and the learner will need much practice, as well as proficiency in slipping, before he attempts it with any seriousness. Let him, and his boxing chum, practise it assiduously.

A leads with his left at the head. B moves his head to his left, just sufficiently to allow of A's glove passing over his right shoulder. Simultaneously with the head movement, B carries his right glove forward, across A's arm from the outside, its objective being A's jaw.

This right cross counter is one of the most severe and punishing of all boxing blows. It has attained a sort of traditional notoriety; and it is hardly ever absent from any fictional description of a fist fight.

But not always does it have the devastating effect the fictionist would try to convince his readers, because there is considerable difficulty, uncertainty anyway, in landing it properly. For absolutely correct timing and perfect accuracy in the line of direction are essential. The smallest failure in either of these respects, and the cross counter fails in its purpose. Should the leader-off raise his arm at all as he realises that his lead has been slipped, the counter will go awry. Or the attacker may carry his head forward—very little is sufficient; and what ought to have been a heavy blow squarely on the jaw, jarring the brain and half dazing the recipient, is reduced to a comparatively ineffective blow on the side of the head.

Fig. 7. Right-hand Cross Counter.

Why the perfect cross counter is so punishing a hit will easily be appreciated. Attacker's head is coming forward with considerable speed at the moment when it receives the impact of the fist, thus adding to the force of the hit; and the counterer,

COUNTER TO LEADS

as he drives his right forward, palm down, elbow brought slightly outwards, rises on his right toes and gets all the added propelling power supplied by the forward movement of the right side of the body with the suddenly straightened right leg behind it. The shoulder is forced forward, and back of it is the whole of the hitting power of the muscles lying around the shoulder.

Practise the right cross counter as much as you can. The mechanical hitting movement may be carried out with the aid of a punching bag or ball, but nothing can take the place of practice with an actual opponent; without his help, the essential feature of accurate timing is impossible. But it is not at all necessary that the helper towards your proficiency should take the risks incidental to such practice. When he leads at you with his left, let him place his open right hand across his face and jaw, and instead of your delivering the counter with firmly closed fist and all your weight behind it, check the force of your blow, so that your hit is met by his glove, held a few inches in front of his face. Then when you have made the blow a few times, you can become attacker and give him the opportunity of practising the counter.

Points to Observe

There are one or two points incidental to the right cross counter not referred to that the learner should observe. As your partner leads at you, and immediately before you slip your head to your left, advance the left foot, up to a dozen inches (to add yet greater force to the blow), and instead of its moving directly forward, let it be slightly to the left. Also, as the right hand goes forward, draw back your left, so that, should the cross

Fig. 8. Left-lead slipped and body counter with right.

counter fail to effect all that you intended, before you take a spring backward, you will be in position for shooting in a left-hand hit at the body.

When you have gained a certain proficiency with the cross counter, do not spoil your chances of using it effectively by too frequent attempts at exploiting it. If tried too often, opponent will

COUNTER TO LEADS

come to anticipate it. Either he will nullify it by dropping his chin as he leads off, so that his left ear is against the inside of his upper arm, thus completely covering his jaw with his shoulder, or he will slightly change the direction of his lead,

Fig. 9. Ducking left-hand lead, combined with left-foot advance outside opponent's left-foot and counter with left at the mark.

aiming for the place that your face will occupy when your slipping of the head is made.

Have nothing to do with the clumsy device advocated by some teachers as a guard against a possible cross counter, which is to bring the right hand up to the face when starting the left lead and so covering the jaw with the glove. The move leaves the body badly exposed and offers the opportunity for a duck under your left hand, a step forward, and a violently driven right-hander under the heart, the blow given a somewhat upward instead of a horizontal direction.

This last is a counter that deserves to be well cultivated; it gives a very heavy and punishing blow, only second in its weakening effects to a drive full on the "mark".

Left-Hand Body Blow Counter

The left-hand body blow counter is somewhat similar. But in this case, as you step in and duck, the latter action is taken to your right, and your glove will be directed towards the pit of the stomach—the famous "Broughton's mark", or "the wind", as the schoolboy calls it.

CHAPTER IV

Feinting: The Double Lead and One-Two

The older school of instructors, who placed their faith in straight hitting, simplified matters by reducing the number of hits to four, viz:—

The left hand at the head;
The left hand at the body;
The right hand at the head;
The right hand at the body.

FEINTING

The Four Attacks

The four hits enumerated are capable of a large number of variations, since any one of them may be used either offensively or defensively, as attacks or counters. With the left hand attack at the head, the situations arising out of it, and the parries and counters proper thereto, we have already dealt. The left hand at the body now requires explanation.

Some of the uses of the left hand body blow, but as a defensive measure, have been described, yet one must not assume that this hit is not to be used as an attack. On the contrary, such an attack is to be well recommended, as judiciously varying the character of your assault, with the result that your opponent is unable to form a forecast of your intentions.

It has been said that a boxing bout is a contest of wits as well as of fists, and a large measure of a boxer's success depends upon his skill in preventing his adversary from calculating correctly just what his opponent means doing. Such skill comes, however, of experience rather than knowledge of the canons of boxing, and the novice cannot expect to possess it.

Feinting

Though it is not possible to teach the novice the knack of foreseeing and forestalling his adversary's intentions, it is possible that he should learn one means whereby the adversary is made to feel uncertain what his vis-a-vis means to do. That means is known as feinting.

The purpose of feinting is to deceive your adversary into assuming that you have the intention of attacking in a certain manner, while your real purpose is something quite different.

"Don't worry about feinting until you've learned how to box," some teachers will advise. And the advice is good up to a certain point. But that point is reached when the novice has learned how to deliver a straight blow and how to defend himself against the same.

"Drawing"

"Drawing" is another means of tricking your opponent by persuading him into delivering or trying to deliver a certain form of attack for which you have already prepared an effective reply.

A feint is a false blow, its purpose to induce opponent to shift his guard and so expose himself to the real blow that follows immediately. A feint may be made as preliminary to a left lead at the head, especially if you have tried the trick previously, drawn your opponent into throwing up his guard, and then hit him in the body. If this happen two or three times, he will not be taken in; he refuses to raise his right arm, and then the feint is converted into a genuine head attack. When this is attempted, the forward step with the left foot should be shorter than in a genuine attack,

FEINTING

to be followed by a further advance when the actual hit is delivered.

A feint at the head should usually precede a left-hand attack at the body; and a duck of the head to the right should accompany the actual blow so as to carry the head outside his left arm in the event of his attempting to retaliate with that weapon. Such retaliation may take the form of an upper cut; so it is well that the attacker should be prepared for this and be ready to guard it by raising his own right and carrying it a trifle outwards.

This upper cut counter (left hand) is a most useful one for the defender, by reason of the fact that a lowering of the body and thrusting forward of the head is a necessary accompaniment to the left lead at the body. Therefore, if leading at the body, you must be prepared to spring back out of danger immediately—a real jump, with the impetus supplied by a spring from the ball of the left foot. The retreat is to be recommended whether the blow get home or is blocked. Thus it will be obvious, even to the learner, that the left lead to the body should never be attempted unless he is sure that he has behind him sufficient room wherein to escape. (Note: Don't bring your head up until you are out of harm's way.)

COUNTERING A LEFT LEAD

Your best guard against a left-hand blow at your body is to meet the oncoming forearm with your open right glove and push it across to your left. The effect of this should be to turn attacker partly round, the whole of his left side open to a severe punch under the arm and at the side of his head with either your left or right. But this may be too much for the novice, who may not have the confidence and time-sense to use it.

The most simple stop is to drop the right arm and, pressing outwards with it, take the force of the blow on the elbow or glove.

If quick, drive forward your left glove as you make the stop, and you will get in a useful counter at attacker's face.

Another defence is to drop the guard arm and step back out of distance.

The ideal means of meeting the left-hand body blow, which the learner may attempt later on, is by means of a stop hit. Its success depends upon your divining attacker's intention combined with perfect accuracy of timing. In making this lead, attacker " gives " his head, and to it you send your left glove before his lead gets home. If well done, your hit takes him full in the mouth just as his glove meets your guard arm.

Conservation of strength and energy are points of successful boxing that the novice cannot begin too early to understand. Therefore, any method by means of which he can spare himself is worth taking a little trouble to master; and the first mentioned of the defences against a left body lead is at once so simple and so effective that he would

FEINTING

do well to practise it carefully until it becomes as automatic as the more usual arm-across-the-body guard.

USING THE RIGHT

The right-hand hit at the head, as an attack, is not to be encouraged; employed as a cross counter, it has already been described. So, too, the right body counter. But wherever there are boxers and boxing, attacks with the right hand will be seen.

The right arm is the more powerful, and young boxers are apt to use it too much, seeing no good reason why their most powerful weapon should be used less than the left. Yet Jem Ward, the old P. R. champion of England, and esteemed a perfect master of science, used to say that the right should be used but once in a contest—" and then it should end it." This, of course, is an exaggeration. For all that, the learner's desire to attack with his right hand should be held in check. When the right is brought into play for offensive purposes, the opening for its use should first have been made by feinting with the left hand. The most useful is a feint at the body followed immediately by the right sent to the chin. When you do hit with the right, be sure that you step into safe distance and hit as quickly as you know how. And bring up the right foot.

To save yourself a probable counter, duck the head to the left as you hit out.

Even if the learner be not eager to use his right,

he will be bound to meet opponents who are, so it is well to know how to receive them. The following are available.

Step back, carrying head and shoulders backward from the hips.

Carry the head to the right and forward ('ware a left upper cut), raising the left shoulder, on which the glove falls or else passes over.

Throw left arm up and outwards, thus effectively preventing the hit reaching you. From position inside opponent's arm, you may now step forward, bringing up rear foot slightly, and drive your own right at his face. This is the novice's best move.

Having successfully used the left to ward off the right attack, and, coming up, replied with a right-hand face or body blow, either spring back out of distance at once, or, keeping the inside position just gained, indulge yourself in a short spell of in-fighting. If you choose the latter, drop the chin on the chest, keep both elbows in at your sides, and with thumbs turned upward, hammer away at adversary's ribs and stomach with both hands, working the shoulder from side to side as you send in your blows. Body punching is far more effective than head hitting, being more weakening, and in a very few seconds you can crowd in a deal of such punishment. Opponent may reply by raising his elbows, arms bent, and "hooking" at the sides of your head.

But be careful that you do not fall into the mistake of bringing your right foot up too far—level with your left. It must always stay behind it.

FEINTING 43

Otherwise, if your opponent keep his head, step back a trifle and get home on you with an upper cut, you will assuredly be knocked down.

If your adversary be a taller boxer than yourself and with a tendency to exploit a longer reach by

Fig. 10. Guard for right at body.

frequent leading at your head with his right, this in-fighting will prove most effective. Be sure you keep your elbows down and hit upward at him; and if he give ground, follow him up until you get him on the ropes.

The right-hand lead at the body should follow

a left feint at the face, and the hit should be delivered at opponent's left ribs.

Defend by lowering and dropping your left arm, so as to take the blow on the outside of it, keeping arm close to your body. You have a good opportunity for hitting with your right at his chin or stomach.

Counter to Swinging Hits

There is one circumstance in which a direct hit at the head with the right hand may be used most effectively. Your opponent has the trick of swinging his left at your head. Reply to this a few times either by stepping back, ducking, or throwing your right up and outward (down and outward if he swing at your body) to parry the blow. The next time he tries it, suddenly send your right (palm down) straight at his jaw, getting a strong push off from your right foot (heel lifted), draw back your left arm, at the same time swinging your left shoulder backward. Your straight blow should arrive quicker than his swing, and if you get home nicely he will remember it.

It is the finest counter to the left-hand swing that can be employed.

Additional to but arising out of the fundamental hits already dealt with, are two forms of attack of great utility—the Double Lead and the One-Two. Though the novice in his earliest stages will not have to trouble himself with these, later he will

FEINTING

want to give them his attention as, correctly applied, they form most disconcerting and effective forms of aggression. Each is the immediate following up of a leading hit by another, but they need to be considered separately for a reason that will be obvious.

In the Double Lead only the left hand is concerned; the One-Two requires both hands.

The Double Lead

To effect this satisfactorily you do not need to be well away from your opponent. The objective of the first hit is opponent's stomach, and to increase the chance of getting the blow home you may first feint a left at the head once or twice so as to get him nervous as to where his next guard will be required. At the proper moment you shoot in your body hit, stepping well in but not rising so much on the right toes as when delivering an ordinary lead. As you feel your glove connect, bring up the rear foot, say, twelve inches; whip up your left glove immediately the punch has gone home and, simultaneously with your right foot completing its advance, aim a second blow—but this time at the face. There must be no hesitation or check in the delivery of the second punch.

Don't forget that in the delivery of both blows the knuckles should be uppermost.

Unless your adversary has checked you with a stop hit in the face from his left (and this you should be ready to prevent with your right as the first lead is made), you will certainly get one blow home, and, with luck, both of them. Be content with the success and the points gained, and at once spring back out of distance.

THE ONE-TWO

This is two blows following immediately upon each other, a straight left, then a straight right, and they form perhaps the most devastating of all attacks. In the old knuckle-fighting days a successful One-Two was frequently the means of finishing the battle out of hand. But no boxer will perform the trick successfully until he has mastered the art of straight hitting and has acquired the shoulder-swinging knack referred to in the description of the left counter following a right guard.

You may send :—Left at body, right at head.
Left at head, right at body.
Both hands at body.
Both hands at head.

The second of these is that with which the learner should first make acquaintance.

Until you are master of the straight right and left, no amount of description will teach you how the One-Two can be made. When you are master, you will need little instruction. Here it is—taken from Jim Driscoll in the ring, Driscoll being one of the very few English boxers of recent times—Dick

FEINTING

Burge was another—who had the One-Two to perfection.

Driscoll never made the common mistake of lesser boxers of trying to make the One-Two a full-power punch with each hand. His left hand at the head was never a particularly severe blow. He did not intend it should be. To make it so defeats the "one-two-er's" purpose. The full-power left at the head sends the body too far over the feet, the left shoulder too far forward, for the following right at the body to be delivered with the rapidity and force intended.

So Driscoll would make his left hand hit little more than a sharp jab, having worked in by degrees (not jumped in) near enough to allow him to get the blow home without his body being carried much beyond the vertical. His left shoulder moved well forward and his right glove was taken back—but not unduly so, certainly not to or even beyond the outline of the ribs, as one sometimes sees in spectacular pictures. His right heel would be scarcely off the floor. Then, immediately the left hit was made, the opening secured, followed a quick raising of the right heel, a straightening of the rear leg and simultaneous swinging of the body from the hips from right to left, completing the throwing of the whole of the body weight behind the thrust-forward right shoulder and fast travelling right arm.

There was no conscious drawing back of the right elbow before the body swing, a fault which is the surest warning to opponent of what is his attacker's intention. The perfect One-Two is the finest illustration possible of the economy of effort with the maximum of result; and when practising it (not so much on the punching ball, which is easy, but on a human adversary), the first part of this description is that which the learner should keep in the forepart of his mind.

As such an attack needs great rapidity of action, successful defence against it also needs to be swift. And having progressed so far, the learner will realise what that defence should be—viz., a straight guard with the right followed by a straight guard with the left.

CHAPTER V

In-fighting

Lovers of the old style of boxing, the "hit, stop, and get away" method, will emphatically assert that modern boxing is spoiled by the prevalence of in-fighting—the result of the adoption of American and Continental tactics; the rush, the wild swinging blows, the clinch.

There may be something in the contention; yet in-fighting is not, as many persons erroneously assume, the same thing as clinching; and in-fighting was a very prominent characteristic of old English dugilism.

IN-FIGHTING

Clinching

The detestable practice of clinching doubtless has had some bearing upon the development of modern in-fighting, but the two things are wholly different; and desperate close-quarter work may take place without either contestant having the smallest desire to clinch.

In-fighting is the natural resort of the boxer of lesser height and reach, and, possibly, the lesser skill, but the superior in sheer bodily strength and determination. Aware that his adversary's greater reach of limb and quickness enable him to be pinked again and again with small hopes of effective return while the game of "long bowls" is continued, it would be surprising if he did not seek the best means of effective retaliation by negativing his opponent's advantages.

In-fighting is not as good to watch as long-distance boxing; but it can be perfectly fair and honest, and it ceases to be so only when it changes to clinching and hanging on.

Were referees in general more strict in dealing with the latter plagues, disqualifying without stint or mercy boxers who had already been warned for the offence, everyone would rejoice, and real in-fighting would meet with the appreciation it merits.

Certainly it would be grossly unfair to deprive the short-armed, sturdily built fighter of the one means by which he can bring his long-armed, quick-hitting adversary down to his own level.

One takes risks in getting to close quarters, and the in-fighter often sustains a good deal of punishment before he gains his object. Once there, if he can follow his man as rapidly as the other tries to get away, he will dominate the situation; for once in, it is a difficult job for the opponent to fight him out of position.

Getting inside is a matter of persistent following up, jumping in, probably with chin lowered and gloves held before the face to take the blows that surely will come. Stepping in to duck under a lead and following up, whether hit or not, will often gain the position. But there is no need to copy the ways of those who make wild, bull-like rushes and try to drive opponent back to the ropes, and keep him there.

Body Hitting

One piece of advice from an old-time teacher I have never been able to subscribe to: " Never fight at the body in in-fighting, invariably make the head your mark." His reminders that the inside position should be obtained and the shoulders twisted towards opponent with each blow given, also to hit rapidly and to bring up the right foot are sound enough, but experience proves that for in-fighting body hitting gives the best results. Such punishment weakens a man, and, after all, the object of boxing is to weaken your opponent as much as possible while taking care that he does not effect this upon yourself.

IN-FIGHTING

But remember in this body hitting that your blows take effect upon the front of the body. Keep away from intentionally hitting at any part of opponent's back; and overcome the temptation to indulge in such illegitimate tricks as locking his arms or holding his gloves, holding with one hand and hitting with the other.

Drawing

Feinting and Drawing are illustrations of what is called "Ringcraft." So important is ringcraft that sometimes it will bring about the defeat of superior skill. But ringcraft cannot be taught—only the mechanical processes that the brainy boxer employs.

Feinting, the threat which disguises your real purpose, has already been mentioned; Drawing is the offering opponent what appears to be a valuable opportunity for scoring and by so doing to expose himself to a punishing rejoinder. It is a most useful asset to the short and strong, but not slow, boxer who is deficient in reach.

The draw for the left lead at the head is accomplished by first feinting with your left, then lowering your head and dropping your guard. The opening is too good to miss, and the man lets fly. This you have been anticipating; so you are ready to slip his glove and counter, either with the left at his head or body, or with your right to his jaw.

Another good draw is to offer the chance of a

right cross counter. Feint with left at head, not too obviously exposing your chin by raising your head, but sufficiently to induce opponent to believe in the opportunity to bring his right across. He does; prepared for it, you turn it aside easily with

Fig. 11. Having drawn a right cross counter, boxer slips head to left and replies with a straight right to chin.

your left or slip your head and, not expecting anything of the kind, he is countered severely with your right.

The boxer addicted to right-hand swinging may be made to fall an easy victim—now and again;

IN-FIGHTING 53

to be continually attempting to draw your opponent, and by the same methods, is poor generalship; he gets awake to your trick, and wary. Feint your right at his head, lowering the left hand, and exaggerating the turn of the body to your left (his right) naturally accompanying a right lead. He sees the opening for his favourite blow. His left has already gone up to parry your right, and round comes his right with all his force. You knew it was coming; your head is slipped under it, and you are in fine position to swing your left shoulder forward and drive in your glove at head or body, whichever seems better, with staggering effect.

There is another draw worth practising since it appears to be so little known, though several of the old school of fighters were most proficient with it. Tempt your opponent into following you up by frequently stepping back out of distance from his leads. He may get the notion you are afraid—at least, that you are dubious as to the quality of your guard and ability to counter. So he follows up—just as you desire. When you are ready, your next retreating gte p is only a feint; instead of carrying back your right foot, to be followed by the left, in the ordinary manner, take a half-step back with the left, not shifting the right at all. Opponent makes his advance, unsuspecting, and at once you dash forward with the left foot first, getting a real spring from the rear, and it will be hard luck indeed if your left does not take him heavily—the attack will be so entirely unexpected.

Tactics

By tactics is meant the manner in which you will use your knowledge and skill to defeat your opponent. Obviously, if you are tall and long-armed you will pursue a different method from that which is best suited to the short, stocky boxer. If the first, long-range boxing, picking up points by means of quick assaults and as quick removals from danger, will be likely to be your best suit, just as hard countering, in-fighting, and feinting will be that of the second type. But you will find also that a stereotyped system of boxing is inadvisable; that you will need to adapt your tactics to the kind of opponent facing you.

The careful, risk-nothing type that stands off and then makes various efforts to trick you into errors and bad positions cannot be dealt with in the same manner as the rushing, neck-or-nothing fighter who bores into you, willing to take punishment on the chance of landing a decisive blow, forces you to the ropes, and evidently hopes to get the bout over in the shortest possible time. The one you will need to tempt into more vigorous action (and so provide you with opportunities); the other—unless you are also of his mind—it will be best to box rather than to fight. You will try to evade or slip his fierce onslaughts, use your greater reach to stab and prod him, and rely on your footwork to prevent his getting you into positions of danger.

A boxing bout is something more than the mere

IN-FIGHTING

exchange and avoidance of punches; it is far from being a mechanical exercise, and mere mechanical perfection of attack or defence will not ensure victory. It is a contest of wits wherein the quicker thinker, the closer observer of his adversary and his methods, is more likely to get the verdict than the man who boxes " by the book."

And if you have all this in your mind, framing your tactics accordingly, remember to give the other fellow the credit of believing that he is thinking much the same as you are. Always it is an asset if you can force your adversary to fight the kind of fight that suits you; and what that is you know best—the best in any given circumstances. Many a good boxer, the better of the pair in the ring, has finished a loser because his opponent's methods have not allowed him the chance to settle down to the kind of boxing that best suits him.

But how to do this no book can teach you—no instructor. You must learn it by experience, by actual boxing; by using your wits as well as your fists and feet.

The Right-Handed Boxer

In Boxing and Fencing, one is always liable to come up against an adversary who does not play exactly as you do. Being of the ordinary type that stands with left foot and left hand advanced, you may easily find yourself faced by an opponent who elects to stand right side forward. The boxer to whom this kind of adversary is new usually finds him more than a trifle disconcerting. It seems to him quite evident that the usual methods do not apply; he is in two minds what to do.

The following suggestions, given by the writer's teachers, may be found useful.

Have as little to do with in-fighting as possible. He will know exactly what he is doing; you are liable to be a trifle bewildered by novelties in the way of attack of which you have no previous experience. A right-hand boxer, he is likely to be a heavy hitter, and at close quarters the advantage will be his.

Work to your own left instead of to the usual right. Your customary left leads will be less effective; do not be lavish with them. Use your own right more freely and make the most of ducking and slipping. If you lead with the right, duck to the left. When he leads with his right, duck to left and hit with right at his body, or slip his lead and cross counter with your left.

His right hand leads you will guard with your left arm; his left arm you will guard with your right just as you would any straight left blow. When you hit with your right at his body, aim rather at the stomach than the ribs or under the heart. But be sure you have your left ready to stop his right. If he hit at your body with his right, either guard by bringing left arm to side, or parry by bringing down left arm to the inside of his right, and counter with the right—preferably at his face or throat, because in hitting at your body he will almost certainly bring his head forward. A right hand upper cut can be made most effectively thus.

If he swing with his right—quite likely—step forward inside his arm, with your left aimed at his face and then, twisting your shoulders, follow with a hard right to the mark.

Don't get flustered and assume that the orthodox hits, etc., that you have learned, cannot be made to apply to the changed position of your opponent.

CHAPTER VI

Training

A lengthy dissertation on training, with advice as to what to eat and drink, what to avoid, how and when to exercise, etc., is as needless as it is apt to be incapable of being carried into effect.

In the first place, the average boxer, pursuing the sport for the enjoyment and physical benefits it provides, has neither the need nor inclination to indulge in any hard-and-fast training rules. These are better suited to the professional exponent. The latter's hard training, intended to take him through a lengthy and exacting contest, is not within the opportunity of the ordinary amateur boxer. If the latter be reasonably fit, his vital organs and muscles in a satisfactory state of use and development, his wind in good order, he will be fully able to get the requisite amount of pleasure and exercise out of his sport.

He knows without telling that heavy cigarette or pipe smoking is not good for the wind; that eating and drinking to excess are obstacles against his doing well in any form of vigorous recreation.

THE WIND

To enjoy boxing the wind must be in good order —which is to say that the lungs must have the opportunity for plenty of exertion beyond the ordinary. Deep breathing exercises taken regularly are valuable, as they increase lung capacity. Skipping—with plenty of fresh air available—is good for both the wind and the legs, but the exercise needs to be taken briskly. An outdoor run now and again, for, say, a couple of miles—not a race, but a comfortable trot—with sixty to a hundred yards bursts at a fast clip sandwiched in here and there, is an excellent means for improving the wind and accustoming the lungs (as they do not get accustomed by the habits of ordinary existence) to increased and sustained effort. But such a run, with an interval between it and the next of four or five weeks, will bring about no worth-while improvement. Once a week should be arranged for.

If the time before breakfast can be found, a

TRAINING

sharp walk up to a half-mile, with a trot back home, the last forty or fifty yards covered at your best pace, taken every morning is of first-class benefit for getting the lungs into proper working order—and keeping them so. If other sports, such as football, wrestling, hockey, are followed during the boxing season, such training runs will add to the player's effectiveness.

W. G. George's Hundred-Up, or stationary running, the motions of ordinary running being performed, the knees well raised, but the feet coming down every time on the same mark, is a satisfactory substitute for skipping.

Long walking is always to be recommended, the pace to be not less than four miles an hour. So is a two or three times a week fast walk of a mile, taking short strides and working the arms up and down. This exercise is excellent for the arms, which tire with maintaining the positions that boxing practice requires.

Muscular Development

The part played by muscular development in boxing cannot be other than interesting to its exponent, and which are the most suitable exercises for increasing that development is a very proper question for discussion.

As has been shown over and over again, the very ✓ strong man with a development of muscle far beyond the ordinary is not invariably the most successful of performers within the ring. That hard-hitting has a very distinct value is not to be gainsaid ; few boxers have made a name for themselves who have not carried " a punch "; but it would be untrue to declare that the boxer with the abnormally developed muscles is necessarily a harder puncher than one whose muscles show a lesser size and definition.

" The stronger you are, the harder you'll hit. It stands to reason," will argue one.

" Muscular development counts for nothing," his opposer will declare. " Look at Jimmy Wilde ! There never was a harder hitter at his weight, and he had no muscular development at all."

The truth must lie somewhere between these two assertions.

If the strength be in the right place ; if it can be quickly brought into action ; if it be allied with the knowledge how to hit—then muscular strength must be an asset ; to increase it must improve the boxer's chances of success.

Wilde was a phenomenon, and his citation proves nothing. He hit tremendously hard ; and this was partly to be accounted for by his wonderful speed, and partly by his equally wonderful timing. Certainly his hitting powers did not depend upon the fact that he carried so little muscle. He hadn't much ; but what there was, was in the right place and he had it under marvellous control.

Other things being equal, the boxer with the better developed hitting muscles, and strong forearms and

TRAINING

wrists, will be a harder hitter than he whose muscular system has had no special training. Strength is a valuable quality, but it must be of the kind that boxing requires; and huge muscles that have been developed by means that aim only at size and take no account of suppleness and elasticity are a hindrance. The slow acting muscle is useless to the boxer, to whom speed is of such great importance. Therefore, any kind of exercise requiring slow and powerful muscular action is to be avoided.

Strength is developed by the overcoming of resistance against muscle action; but that resistance must not be of such a degree that it is to be overcome only by slow and ponderous effort.

Strength will be developed by the lifting of heavy weights, and devotees of heavy weight lifting assert that their exercise is useful to the boxer. They declare that speed is not absent from heavy weight lifting; on the contrary, that speedy movements are a necessity for their pastime and are developed by its practice. Maybe, but the kind of strength that lifting heavy weights develops is emphatically not the kind the boxer requires, and he will be very ill advised if he turn to weight lifting as a form of muscular training.

The kind of strength developed by use of heavy weights is the kind most unsuitable for boxing. The weight lifter's muscles are trained to perform a few extraordinarily vigorous movements of a set character; that these are individually quick movements is beside the point. Such kind of strength is useless for boxing. There must be enduring strength, capable of lightning-like action. There can never be the same violent concentration of effort in boxing as in weight lifting. The boxer's muscles are in a state of continuous movement, yet none of these movements will be of a set, stereotyped kind. He is required to perform them an infinite number of times. Let the weight lifter attempt to emulate him, and he will find that his much larger, stronger muscles, trained to a different purpose, will tire the quicker. The " strong man " type is not the boxing type.

THE BEST EXERCISES

All physical exercises then should be of a free, loosening character, acting on joints as well as muscles and keeping these loose. A few resistance exercises, calling into play the hitting muscles—those at the back of the arms, around the shoulders, from the shoulder down the ribs, and the upper chest muscles to a more limited degree—will be useful. Boxing practice, use of the punch ball, some wrestling for all-round toughening work, are to be recommended. Gymnastic apparatus work should be taken to only a limited extent. Cycling and boxing do not go well together.

There is one part of his body where the development of muscle will be of great use to the boxer—the middle trunk region. Usually this is a very neglected

TRAINING 63

part; few men have these muscles well developed unless they have received a special preparation. Such is well worth while. These muscles are in almost continuous use during a boxing bout, though the boxer may not be conscious of the fact. Little used in the ordinary way, lacking in strength and stamina, they will tire quickly.

Further, a good, solid development of the abdominal and stomach muscles affords the best possible protection against the effect of severe blows in this region. By no means should the boxer neglect the development of these muscles. He will do well to devote a few minutes every day to their particular development.

He should indulge in every variety of body bending, turning, twisting, and stretching exercises. Touching the floor with his hands, knees straight, then rising and bending well back. Turning the body at the waist, hips kept firm, from right to left and back again. Side body bending, hips firm, knees straight, with one arm stretched above the head, the other stretched downwards. Combinations of turning with twisting.

Floor exercises for the stomach, abdominal, and back muscles are:—

Lying on back, legs together, hands back of head, a small weight (at first), say, a cushion, across the feet, then rising to sitting position and bending well forward, heels not to leave the ground. Lower to starting position and repeat.

From same position, raise legs alternately and

carry above and down towards the body, keeping them straight. When used to this exercise, both legs may be worked together, and carried so far above the body and downwards as to allow the toes to touch the floor behind the head.

Bending knees (same starting position) and bringing them close in to body, followed by quick straightening and return to starting position.

From same position, raise legs above body and make rapid cycling movements with feet and legs.

Kneeling on floor, arms behind, bend forward so as to bring forehead as close to floor as possible, rise and bend well back.

The familiar " on the hands down " exercise.

Never Forget

To have your eyes always open—also on your opponent.

To keep your mouth always closed.

To keep control of your temper.

To give no sign that a blow has hurt. To know he has landed a damaging punch encourages your opponent.

To keep strictly to the rules.

When in a competition, and however bad you may be feeling, that your opponent is probably in the same state—perhaps worse. So keep your hands up and *see it through* !

www.ingramcontent.com/pod-product-compliance
Lightning Source LLC
Chambersburg PA
CBHW031322150426
43191CB00005B/300